GOOD GRIEF

A COMPANION TO CHANGE AND LOSS

DIPTI TAIT

BALBOA.
PRESS

A DIVISION OF HAY HOUSE

Balboa Press books may be ordered through booksellers or by contacting:

Balboa Press
A Division of Hay House
1663 Liberty Drive
Bloomington, IN 47403
www.balboapress.com
1 (877) 407-4847

Print information available on the last page.

ISBN: 978-1-5043-5029-7 (sc)
ISBN: 978-1-5043-5031-0 (hc)
ISBN: 978-1-5043-5030-3 (e)

Library of Congress Control Number: 2016902254

Balboa Press rev. date: 3/2/2016

ACKNOWLEDGEMENTS

For Ram and Manju Paul
I thank you both from the bottom of my heart for being kind,
loving and supportive parents raising me to be
independently strong, self-sufficient and disciplined.
I love and miss you both and dedicate this book to you.

Thank you to my incredibly inspiring Hypnotherapy lecturer David Newton for training me in the wonderfully invaluable Solution Focused Model of Hypnotherapy that I use in my work and incorporate into my daily life.

Thank you Jackie Mendoza, my wonderful writing coach, you kept me firmly on the (often) difficult track, and helped me remain motivated and inspired enough to get all the way to the end.

Thank you Kate Ingarfield for your time and effort reading through the first draft carefully and giving me your detailed notes and helpful comments.

Thank you Sarah Steele, for your fantastic copy editing skills and being an invaluable text support service. I'm so sorry about all the annoying double spaces after every full stop!

Many thanks to my focus group for the feedback. (You know who you are)

Thank you to the very talented Vanessa Mendozzi for the brilliant cover design, you took my vision and effortlessly created a perfect cover for me.

Thank you to my very special and wonderful boys, Krishan and Jacob, for reminding me of my own important role as a mother, and for teaching me valuable lessons that only you, as my children can teach me. I am so very proud of you both, and love you from the bottom of my heart.

Finally... Toby ~ thank you for being my rock.

You are *very* special to me. I am so grateful for your presence in my life.

Thank you for believing in me, even when I don't. I am so lucky to have you, and I love you more and more with every single day that passes.

FOREWORD

This book, born out of death, is a compilation and collection of my life's musings. Within it I share the story of personal loss in my life and how I have moved towards a place of acceptance. It is by no means meant to be a bible for how to do things or how to process things, but it is *my* process, and maybe my way will inspire you to discover your own way. My hope for this book is to become a life and death support for you and it is my contribution to your healing from grief.

I hope by sharing my personal experiences within my own healing journey, you know you are not alone and feel comforted in your time of change and loss. I hope to make this book a metaphorical friend that you can pick up and put down at your pace. I hope you pick it up and flick through it when you need a shoulder to lean on, or a boost.

You will stumble upon the right section, paragraph or chapter and you will know that you are not alone. You are grieving. It's a natural process, like the tides that come in and out on the shore of the ocean of your consciousness. Some are high; some are low. It's about learning how to surf the waves of grief and not drown in the intense sorrow of loss.

CONTENTS

1 Saying Goodbye To My Mother 1
2 The Adjustment Period 11
3 The Seven Stages Of Grief 17
4 Write Your Emotions Out Of Your Head 21
5 Lonely In A Crowded Room 27
6 After Death There Is Growth 31
7 Saying Goodbye To My Father 37
8 Saying Goodbye To Myself 43
9 The After Shock 49
10 Guilt Is The Bad Cop 53
11 Sadness Is Like A Sickness 57
12 Denial And Acceptance 61
13 Anger Increases Our Strength 63
14 The Stress Bucket 69
15 The Three Ps 75
16 The Imagined Lemon 79
17 Moving Into Emotional Intelligence 83
18 The No/Yes Principle 87
19 The Onward Journey 93

Notes To Self 98

1

SAYING GOODBYE TO MY MOTHER

The night-nurse gently shook me awake and softly said, 'It's time.' I nodded, slightly groggily, allowing the enormity of those two little words to sink in. I took a deep breath in and sat up, my eyes adjusting to the dimly lit room. The room was a familiar one: it was my mother's bedroom. The one she had slept in since I was five years old. She had slept alone for the past 15 years, my mum was widowed – she had lost her husband, my darling dad, to cancer. I had also been there with him as he passed away, which made me feel like quite the expert at saying good bye to a parent, but in this case, past experience doesn't seem to be much consolation.

I walked over to my mother's bed on the other side of the room and looked down at her tiny sleeping frame. She was breathing, gently, but very deeply. Her breathing had changed ever so slightly from when I kissed her goodnight several hours before. I felt very contemplative as I thought about letting my mother go. I also thought about myself as a daughter. In a few moments, I would also have to let go of the idea that I am a daughter.

My thoughts were gently brought back into the present moment by Comfort, which unbelievably, yet ironically was the name of the Marie Curie nurse who stood by my side. She held my hand and gave it a reassuring squeeze and asked if I was 'ready'. I paused for a moment deliberating this interesting choice of word. I decided it was a good word. If she had asked me if I was 'fine' or 'alright', this would have been odd, but for me to prepare for what was about to happen, of course I had to be 'ready'.

I swallowed back the lump in my throat and squeezed my tears back into their tear ducts. I looked up and flashed her a brave smile. 'Yes,' I nodded, 'How much time have we got?' I managed to whisper. She cocked her head as if to indicate not very much. I asked if I had enough time to light some candles and burn some incense. She understood and urged me to be as quick as I could.

I stepped away and kissed my mother's ever so slightly furrowed forehead. It was very soft and warm and I knew that it wouldn't be much longer before the warmth subsided.

In the next room, I collected the candles and the incense burner and this momentary distance allowed me to compose and prepare myself for what was about to happen. Reality was fast looming and smacking into me like a train on a track. The time had come to finally say goodbye. My mum was actually leaving me. This was the moment I had been dreading, but not quite believing.

My mother had been given the diagnosis of terminal liver cancer over 18 months previously. She was a hugely optimistic person, and did not want to hear any talk of her life expectancy, so we did not find out 'how long she had left'. Because of this uncertainty, I'm not sure I had taken the 'terminal' part of the illness seriously until this actual moment, as I lit one scented tea-light after another. I quickly filled the room with candlelight, and as the woody vanilla aroma swirled around the room, it created a calm, relaxing and meditative atmosphere. I put her soft mantras on in the background and came back to hold my mother's hand. I closed my eyes and for the first time said a 'real' prayer, to a 'real' god. Unlike my agnostic father, my mother had held traditional Hindu beliefs of god, reincarnation, the soul and karma, and it felt right for me to step into her belief system in this moment to be in the same thought space as her. I silently asked god for her guides, angels and loved ones in spirit to come and get her when she was ready and I informed them that I was ready to facilitate her soul liberate itself from the physical world and her dying body.

I wanted the ambience to be just right, just how she would have wanted and expected it.

The room was silent, apart from the soft music playing, beautifully peaceful and calm and there was an air of expectancy. I held my face close to my mother's cheek and could feel her ebbing breath against my own tear-stained cheek. Her breath was still warm and smelt slightly of minty mouthwash.

I closed my eyes and knew that it was time to say goodbye. I told her in my mind over and over how much I loved her. I was sorry for everything I needed to be sorry for, and I loved her, and I would miss her; the children loved her, they would miss her; and I hoped her soul's onward journey would be peaceful; and I loved her, and I really loved her, and I was sorry. After a few minutes of this nonsensical giddy repetition, my instincts dictated that I lift my head to kiss her, and as I did, she took her final breath of air and then exhaled very slowly almost like she had a slow puncture. I watched her brow instantly un-furrow and every muscle in her face relax. Her expression was peaceful, and she appeared to have an ethereal glow about her. Her fingers uncurled out of my grip and it was over, that was it, she had gone.

No drama, no bells and whistles, nothing. Just an empty shell left behind. My mother was no longer inside her body.

Comfort squeezed my hand again, which was still clutching on to my mother's limp soulless hand and then stepped outside the room, leaving me alone with my disbelief and my mother's lifeless body. I just stared at her blankly immobilised and frozen. My emotions and breath seemed to have also escaped me. I was helpless, numb, empty and hollow. I felt like I had also left my body and I somehow became a detached observer floating over this extremely surreal tableau. I continued to silently stare at this body that only a few moments ago contained my own mother. The body that, as I remembered from my father's passing, would be cooling down rapidly, and would only take a few minutes to turn to cold stone.

I placed a soft kiss goodbye on her smooth forehead, knowing that this would be the last warm kiss I would be able to feel and allowed the tears to flow. But suddenly, they had all dried up as if I had in that moment also turned to stone.

The first realisation that went through my mind was 'I am an orphan.' I cannot describe easily the sudden feeling of loneliness and desperate isolation that came over me, but this feeling triggered a distant memory and I was instantly transported back into my childhood.

> I was alone, in the dark, bobbing around; maybe even spinning ... It was hard to tell. I was in a space with no obvious boundaries. I may have even been floating, or sinking – there was no point of reference. It was very dark, pitch black. It almost felt as if I had turned my vision around to stare inside my own brain and witness my own thoughts flickering on and off in the distance. Like when you have your eyes shut tightly and eventually pulsating balls of colour and lights seem to permeate the filmy eyelid that usually blocks the outside world to the retina's scrutiny. Was I dead? There was a heavy silence, a silence that was so irritatingly loud, it was almost deafening. It felt like I had no body, almost like being in a flotation tank that is exactly the same temperature as your body. Suspended, in space, in mid air? Where was I? I couldn't shout; I had no voice. There was no one to hear me,

even if I could. How did I get here? How do I
get out? What should I do? What could I do?
I could wait. I surrendered to the stillness. A
rhythmic reverberation punctured the stillness.
What was that? I listened and felt. It was a beat.
A heartbeat. I waited, until it was time. Time
for what? All these questions! Who was I asking
them to? Myself? Who was answering them?
Me? Was I having a dialogue with myself? I
realised, yes, I was. I was thinking, and this
was all I was. I was a thought, a seven-year-
old thought. A seven-year-old thought with a
beating heart.

This was a recurring dream of mine. I had it on a regular
basis and always woke up feeling the loneliness lingering.
This particular memory recall triggered more memories, as
if I were watching a cinema projection in my mind of my
own life. It felt very surreal, not dissimilar to the reports one
hears of near-death experiences, where people have their life
'flash before them'. It was as if I too was scanning through my
life's timeline. Searching for a point of reference, a nugget of
familiarity, a moment of comfort. I wanted to be held, cuddled
and supported. I wanted my mummy and daddy back. I wanted
to be back in my mother's womb, all warm, protected and safe.
I needed that feeling of comfort and security. Suddenly, my life
was feeling very slippery, very fluid. I felt like I was melting,
melting back into the foetal position.

My new status as a 38-year old orphan brought with it a
rush of memories and family fable about my own birth, and it
seemed important to recall how my mother had brought me
into the world.

Good Grief

I was my parents' only child and certainly made an extremely interesting entrance into the big wide world. I came into my physical body 12 weeks earlier than expected, kicking and screaming and demanding constant attention from all those around me, from the first moment of my very premature infancy.

Every hour, from the artificially lit incubator in the corner, I would wail 'Allah, Allah' when hungry, much to the amusement of my Hindu mother, who was regrettably unable to place me lovingly upon her bosom, but instead dutifully pumped her expressed milk down a plastic tube fed through my nasal passage into my tiny tummy, the size of a cherry, that would be satisfied after only a minute.

As an only child, losing my parents felt incredibly painful, as there was no one else that shared my pain or deep sense of parental loss. I felt I needed to hold on to the story of my own beginnings, because as one part of my world and identity felt like it was crumbling under the ground I stood on, the other part – the story, felt like it became even more important to hold on to like a helium balloon to help lift me up and keep me safe.

I was nearly not my parents' daughter. I would like to tell you the story of my birth as it was told to me and at many a dinner party whilst growing up. As children we cherish and hold stories dear and true to our hearts, whether these may be comforting bedtime stories, fantastic fairy tales, fables with a moral message or simply our own personal story of who we are.

Stories shape us, and as a solution focused hypnotherapist, I believe very strongly in the power of positive metaphor as a medicine for the mind. If we can learn to create a story that helps encourage our mind to replay the positive story back with compassion, this can be the glue to help us piece together the grief-filled cracks.

7

My birth story became such an embellished family tale, that I sometimes wonder how much of it is true. The story goes like this:

> Three months before I was due, my mum attended her routine maternity hospital check up. My dad was fast asleep in bed, just having done a night-shift, it was that day that I decide to make an early and very unexpected appearance. I am a tiny doll of a baby, weighing just over two pounds. My poor mother was totally confused and my dad, completely unaware that he was now a father. My mum was told that they needed to whisk me away to be incubated, because of infection risks and pre-natal 'complications', and congratulated her on the birth of her baby boy. (Yes, you read that right ... They told her she had had a baby boy!)
>
> So, the news breaks of this tiny baby boy born too soon, into a see-through box. The visitors have to be deterred – a four-day quarantine has been sanctioned due to the potential infection risk to my immature immune system that is already in deep shock. Eventually, after the four days were over, my proud, and undeniably anxious, father gets to meet me – his new son. What a proud moment! Or was it? When presented with what seemed a tiny bundle of white shawl, poking out a tiny wrist brandishing the hugest-looking hospital band marked 'Pre-Natal Female', he nearly drops me, exclaiming, 'This is the wrong

baby.' The nurses look puzzled and slightly amused as the panicking Indian gentleman looks at them in horror and exclaims, 'We had a boy. This label says it's a girl.'

What a mix-up. As it turns out, I was the right baby, and yes, I was a girl. Apparently, my unusually long umbilical cord was stupidly mistaken for a male part of the human anatomy, resulting in the midwife announcing in haste to my also confused mother, the birth of a baby boy, as they hurried me away to intensive care immediately after my unannounced entrance. Slightly worrying, and would in these days it would be a cause for litigation and press coverage, I am sure. But, back then, just a communication error, and a simple apology sufficed.

The two foot by one foot plastic box that became my home for the first four months of my life was warm, relatively comfortable and clean. It wasn't five star accommodation, by anyone's standards, but it was adequate, and served my needs – I couldn't really complain. The room service was faultless, my meals were always on time, and my bed changed on a daily basis. The lights were bright, day and night. Two long fluorescent tubes above my box-shaped bed seemed to have a language of their own – a hum, or a buzz, depending on their mood. The energy contained within them would spark and react at such speed, that this caused the light to dim and flicker. They seemed to be communicating to me. 'You are like us,' they would hiss and buzz to me. 'You are light, a little sparkle of light.' And, funnily enough, that's what I became, my name derived from the Hindu festival of lights, Dipawali, or Diwali, for short.

So that was how my mother saw me into the world, and now I had just seen her on her way out of it, and as she passed away from me, so did the last person who had been there when I was born. When we lose a parent, therefore, we not only lose their physical presence, but our shared experience, and a part of our story disappears into history. All we have left are our memories and these become the very poignant invisible stitches that hold the delicate fabric of our world together.

2

THE ADJUSTMENT PERIOD

You may have this book in your hands because you have also faced, or are about to face a deep loss, or something has changed or shifted in your world in some way or another and you are not sure how to deal with it. This may have been a recent event, or you could be harbouring a residual feeling of not being 'quite right' that you are looking to shake off. Either way, you are in the right place. This book will help.

Grief is not just something that you go through when somebody dies: there are many other experiences that can trigger grief. It may be you are facing a life-changing health issue that you have to come to terms with, or have lost something or someone you held dear, perhaps even the loss of your independence in some way. And it is not only loss that can bring about feelings of grief either – any change to a routine and way of life or way of being can do this. Maybe you are grieving your single life. Becoming a parent, not able to become a parent, miscarriage, abortion, getting married, not being able to find the 'one' for you, unhappy relationships, getting divorced, moving house or location, children leaving home, settling into a new environment, promotion, demotion, redundancy or retirement. Even loss of a pet or best friend, all these life and death experiences can trigger different kinds of grief.

I was talking to somebody recently who told me of his realisation that he was grieving his youth. A forty-something man who had just reunited with friends from 'back in the day', the stories and reminisced encounters from his late teens had instantly transported him back to the early nineties, and for him, these were the golden times, the hedonistic days and nights that merged into one, where he and his friends were young, free and single. They didn't have any responsible cares in the world apart from working out where the next party was going to be held and how they were going to get there. These are the kinds of experiences and times that we grieve. As time ticks on, and passes us by, we remember the past, quite often the best bits that cannot be re-created or reinacted, and we grieve the parts that made us feel good, feel better and most of all feel alive. If we had the ability to erase our memories, we may be able to also erase our grief. But, we need our memories; these keep us safe, so as a by-product, we have to accept the grief as well.

Changes, big and small, in our lives can contribute to feelings of anxiety and stress and can often lead to a grieving process, and this book is designed to support you through these feelings and this process, so you feel understood, you feel nourished and most of all you feel that you are most definitely not alone.

In this book, I examine this 'adjustment period' that I am calling 'grief'. My experience is that we all go through a period of grief with every adjustment we have to make. Even tiny changes can bring about huge shifts in our state, and this book is also a 'survivor's guide' to coping with these changes and losses. The grieving process will still surface, but we may be completely unaware of it happening. Once we acknowledge our grieving, no matter how big or small, this seems to create a neural pathway inside our brain towards a feeling of acceptance, which is one of the final stages of grief and enables us to move on with our lives in a healthy and holistic way.

Losing someone, or something you held very dear to you, is always going to feel like a wrench, on so many levels. I hope to help you understand some of these levels and support you through your tsunami of emotions, thoughts and confusion, and wish to firstly express my condolences to you and offer my deepest sympathy for what you are going through. I have been there myself, and have come through the other end, and this book is a testament to my journey and how I did this.

I have created this book in such a way that it is designed to be portable. I hope it will be a friendly resource (a companion) that you can carry around with you and use as a tool to help you through this difficult transition into acceptance, which is the ultimate destination if any self-healing is to occur.

If it's useful for you, there are a few blank **Note to Self** pages at the end, for you to write any of your personal notes or journal any meaningful insights that you want to remember. These are for you to refer back to and add to whenever you feel like it, as they will become your own healing notes to yourself as you go through this book.

A grieving period is individual to the person who grieves. It has its own shape, form and identity based on belief systems, personal experiences and our own unique programming. However, even though grief is a personal journey and can be so different and changeable varying greatly from person to person, it also has a consistent thread that runs through it which holds it together.

This thread is like a very silky, almost transparent connection that unites us all. We as human beings, although different and unique, all possess the same systems of feeling, thinking and being. We share the pain and sorrow of losing our loved ones, things we held dear or experiences we loved, and we also share the panacea. The panacea is the process that we know to be grief.

The well-known phrase 'a change is as good as a rest' is something that I would like to challenge. I want to highlight the small print that these words need attached to them. Although this phrase may seem innocuous and unassuming, it assumes rather a lot. It suggests that if we want to feel rested and relaxed, all we have to do is simply change the setting. However, it does not take into account that with every change we make, we are also letting something else go, and sometimes when we haven't acknowledged this 'letting go', we feel anxious, and not very rested at all!

In terms of a lovely relaxing break away from the stresses and strains of our everyday lives, a change definitely *can* be as good as a rest. But, if you thrive on the routine and organised structures of your daily life, it can take a few days of unwinding before you can get into the flow of the less frenetic pace of your break away, and then a few days winding yourself back up to re-join the pace of your lifestyle. We are not creatures that react robotically to change; we have to acknowledge the change by understanding what grief is.

A reminder to you that grief is not something we go through only when a loved one dies: it's a process that we can go through on a daily basis, or when a major change happens. The assimilation process can be something that takes some time to filter into our being and is something that we must be patient with and allow to infuse its way in and out naturally.

3

THE SEVEN STAGES OF GRIEF

There are two voices in this book. One is the 'heartfelt' personal experience of my own personal losses and the grieving journey they have taken me on, and the other voice is the awareness of the stages of grief that my 'head' can use as a rough guide to reference and understand the process I am going through. The two voices can sometimes feel opposing: one is overly emotional and the other one is hugely analytical. It's my way of showing you how all of us have these two options, and this book highlights polarised processing, and attempts to show you how to utilise the two voices efficiently.

As I process my own grief, I write in my grief journal, which I have divided into seven stages. I have categorized these stages that I experienced, and will refer to them within this book. The seven stages of my own grief are:

- Shock
- Anger
- Denial
- Loneliness
- Sadness
- Guilt
- Acceptance

Even though this book is about dealing with all the different types of grief we have to face in our lives, it is the actual grieving of a lost loved one that seems to move and shake us the most. I will therefore start with death, as this is something that I have personally had to experience and face extremely close up.

Death really does shake our worlds, as we know them. Through witnessing death, first hand or on a global scale, we are reminded of the fact that we are not indestructible, or physically immortal. We are not here for ever, and nor are our friends or family, and we perhaps then start to question how we live and how we spend our time; our relationships; our values; and our 'place' in society. We start to examine whether or not we are making a valuable contribution to life. We can become introspective and contemplative, but also can become extremely anxious and overwhelmed with the fact of life that is simply known as 'death'.

The grieving process when someone dies is not only about the loss that we face in the relationship, but it is also about the gain in awareness of the bigger picture of ourselves and our own value or standing in society. It's as though a big mirror has been held up to us in our own life to force us to look at our reflection and question who we are, what we stand for and whether we can hold up our heads when the day comes for us to make our own inevitable exit. Of course, when that time comes, we would hope to feel happy and complete, and know that we lived to the best of our abilities.

These questions are all part of the grieving process and are useful tools to understand, not only within ourselves, but also in observing the universal laws of nature that govern us, such as the contrasts of seasonal change.

4

WRITE YOUR EMOTIONS OUT OF YOUR HEAD

When I felt that I was going through a particular stage of grief, I would write in a diary. I labelled the chapters according to the emotions that I discovered were consuming me. I would turn to the relevant section and write, and write and write, in a stream of consciousness until the raw emotions and gut-wrenching feelings of desperation and suffering had subsided. I wrote my grief and poured it out into a barrage of words. Sometimes a tsunami of emotions would flood out on to the page, where my hand could not keep up with the amount that needed to be discharged.

Each time it felt like being in full body labour. The pain was so intense and so excruciating, that all I could do was allow it out and relinquish the grief that was causing my insides to contract. It was forcing me to expel, to release, to give birth. It's an exhausting process, but like childbirth, it's worth going through, because at the end you come out a new you.

Writing your own grief diary can be a very helpful way for you to allow your emotions a safe and measured 'exit strategy'. Our emotional mind is an interesting place: it can feel like an untamed, wild animal that has been caged up and suddenly let out. Our emotions, if we are not careful, can escape and bounce around our head until we feel exhausted with the intense energy of them. By allowing yourself some quiet time to discharge the emotions, incrementally as they come up, by 'writing them out of your head', this can sometimes ease the pressure and prevent them from building up like a time bomb and exploding in an unexpected way.

I don't want you to allow the pollution of bad grief to seep into your emotions, your thoughts and your bodies and start to entangle its poison into your system, your structure and your framework. I want you to be aware, ready, armed, equipped and supported enough to be able to turn the bad grief into good grief. We need to catch this bug before it becomes viral. The only thing I would like to see go viral, is this message.

This is the opening of a poem that Canon Henry Scott-Holland read out in his sermon following the death of 68-year-old King Edward VII in 1910. I also read this poem as part of the eulogy at my father's memorial service 88 years later. I want to share it with you, as it means so much to me and it provided me some comfort while I faced some of the stages of grief – loneliness in particular:

> Death is nothing at all.
> I have only slipped away to the next room.
> I am I and you are you.
> Whatever we were to each other,
> that, we still are.

This sermon must have caused some controversy in its time and, to this day, probably still does, depending on certain belief systems and traditional cultural differences. Whilst I understand that death may not be anything more than what it is – a natural event that occurs to keep the life balance on our planet – the effect of death on the lives of those left behind can be utterly crushing, and it is this very effect that governs us as a society, and trickles down into our thoughts, actions and behaviours.

Why are we not taught how to process death, how to deal with it and how to live with it? I have often wondered whether there is a mechanism or a panacea that we could use or consume to eliminate the suffering that is associated with death?

My wonderings have led me to believe there is. This panacea, in my opinion is actually the opportunity to grieve. When we learn that grief is *normal*, that it is something that goes hand in hand with death, like a bright sunny day inevitably causes dark shadows, we move into a place that acknowledges this concept into our lives and invite it in without fear of it taking over and eating away at our rational mind.

As I write this, I am a 42-year old, British-born Asian female, an only child, a divorced mother of two teenage boys, a self-employed writer and solution-focused hypnotherapist. I am a non-smoking vegetarian, a UK taxpayer and do not have a specified religion and my sexual orientation is heterosexual.

These are the stickers, labels and words that have been tattooed on to me, almost like a second skin, that I wear. It's my uniform, my identity that shapes me and defines who I am dictating my place in this society that I currently live in.

I have one more unusual, extremely sticky substance stuck to me. This substance has one intention only and that is to get my attention. This sticky substance is a lot like a rapidly growing ivy plant – it is called grief. It is incredibly difficult to remove cleanly without messing up everything it makes contact with. It is my emotional response to the loss I face. It is all consuming; eating up my thoughts; intoxicating my spirit. I cannot function; I cannot feel. I am numb. I ache; I suffer; I am in exquisite pain. I cry silent tears; I want to die. I ask the constant question of what is worse – grieving a death or death itself?

Death, as well as life, connects us all. It happens to and surrounds all of us, all the time. It doesn't matter who you are, what you do, where you come from, how much money you have or don't have, what gender or race you are, how old you are, or what your circumstances are – none of us is immune from death, and the loss we are faced with. Each of these 'endings' seems to automatically generate a little sticky label that we call 'grief'.

GOOD GRIEF

I have come to understand that if this little label is dismissed, ignored or pushed away, it, like the ivy plant, will spread and grow and take over if we do not trim it back. It will take over our lives and one day it will consume us, engulf us and attempt to suffocate us in its vice-like grip.

This is why I wanted to write this book. If I can help even one person and throw a pair of secateurs their way, for them to cut themselves free from this sticky tangle, then all that I have been through will be worth it.

I have been so consumed by my own grief, that what I desperately needed was reassurance it was 'normal'. I wanted to hear that I was not going mad, that I was just going through a process, like clothes in a washing machine: it has to go through all the cycles, even the 'spin your world around and around', then finally 'drain' you of everything you possess, before rinsing you clean and ready to hang out to dry. I wanted to be held and supported and understood. I wanted a resource that I could turn to, to know that it would all pass and I would get through it. I needed support, but I didn't want to be a burden. I needed to talk, but I didn't want to be heard. I wanted a hug, but I couldn't be touched. I was in a state of absolute paradox. I was not myself. I needed help, but didn't want to admit it openly.

This can be a common reaction in our British culture, where we are encouraged to 'Keep Calm and Carry On', to put on a brave face and keep on smiling. So, that's what I did. I kept smiling, and the smile became a mask I wore over the pain, sorrow and bitterness. But then one day, the mask cracked. It revealed an ugly grimace that I saw staring back at me in the mirror. I realised then that the mirror was my friend: it was showing me the truth, and making me confront this mask I was wearing and ask the question of myself of whether I wanted to cover up the grimace with heavily contoured make-up or bare

25

all, confront it, process it and bring back my genuine smile. I decided to look deeply into the mirror and ask for help. The magic mirror on the wall told me to write this book.

When I began this book, I didn't know whether I wanted to write a reference book as a guide to coping with grief and loss. When I thought about this, it didn't seem to sit right with me. I felt that I needed to share my whole story as a way of healing and helping. As a solution-focused hypnotherapist I am passionate about helping my clients reach their own states of empowerment and believe that feeding someone a fish is nice, but teaching someone to fish has much greater benefit. (Not if you are a vegetarian of course!)

I write as a cathartic vent. Whenever I feel the need to process something in my life, I find that it helps me if I write it down, so I can become a detached observer of my life. I look at the page from a different perspective. The thoughts going around in my head are no longer muddled and confused but displayed in front of me in an ordered and organised fashion – that, to me, brings some clarity and useful insight.

5

LONELY IN
A CROWDED
ROOM

Birth and death can often create the illusion of isolation and separation. We arrive into this planet on our own, and we depart on our own. Even though we are on our own through these transitions, we are also very much connected to each other, through our thoughts, feelings and attachments. Sometimes, we mistake the feelings of loneliness for a belief that we are suffering silently, and we forget that we as human beings are inextricably linked and similar in many ways, and quite often recognise ourselves in other people all the time as we navigate our way through our lives. We believe and convince ourselves that we are the only people on the whole planet who have ever felt these lonely thoughts, and tell ourselves that nobody can possibly understand these feelings, relate to these feelings or have experienced them themselves.

When we are in the grip of loneliness, we shut ourselves away and pull the duvet over our heads and hide. We want to be hidden in the dark and don't want to be found. When we are in this state, we actually confirm to ourselves that we are alone, and validate the feelings of isolation, having concealed ourselves so well. Nobody seems to reach out to us, or even if they do, we ignore them, shut them out and pull the duvet tighter; making no sounds that might lead to our being found. We are now most definitely alone.

This of course is not true, we are not alone, and when we force ourselves to reach out for help, even in the smallest way, we receive it and we slowly begin to make connections and links and start to realise and remember that we are not isolated, that there is support out there and we can begin again to turn our faces towards the hope, the light, the solutions and the healing.

When you insist on being left alone, and then wonder why it's so lonely, I want you to remember that there is help. This book is with you in those times. It's not a person, or something that you have to explain anything to, and it certainly won't require anything from you. There is no pressure to be anything other than what you are. This book is just a reminder to you that you are most definitely not alone, and when you are ready to emerge from the cave there will be something positive to greet you, hold your hand and guide you along another step up towards your healing.

The desperate feeling of isolation can be completely consuming. As I write this, I am feeling this stage again. I thought I'd done this one and checked it off my list, but of course, we all know that it doesn't work like this.

Grief is most definitely *not* a linear process - It's a full-bodied, kaleidoscopic, multi-dimensional experience. You can see, hear, feel, think, taste and even smell it. It's total sensory overload, and this is what takes us by complete surprise: the tsunami of emotion that bowls you over when you least expect it. Even in the busiest of rooms, and the liveliest of places, you can feel lost, alone and just completely separate from the rest of the humanity and the planet as a whole.

Even though our 'reasoning mind' knows that we are not alone, the 'emotional mind' can be such a powerful shadow that casts its blackness over everything. The colours are dulled, the temperature is lowered and the air is dampened. Suddenly, your bright and summery day has taken a turn for the worse: you open up your curtains to the world and a cold, drizzly, wet, grey uninspiring day has taken its place.

6

AFTER DEATH THERE IS GROWTH

As soon as we are born, like a seed that has been planted and provided with the right conditions, we are subjected to growth and change. We grow in so many ways, major and minor, that to list each form of change would be a mammoth task! On a very basic level, we grow physically, which is an obvious example. Our cells divide, multiply, regenerate and join up to create new tissue, new organs, new bones and new muscles. Even when we stop growing physically, our hair, nails and cells continue to multiply and change state, which does not end until the sophisticated mechanisms that govern this evolution come to a halt. While we are alive, these changes continue to happen and are something that we accept and live with.

We also grow mentally. Our brain has the capacity to evolve, to restructure and totally reprogramme itself (quite often unconsciously). The grey matter contained within our skulls is so unbelievably complex that even leading neuroscientists admit that they don't know all of its functionality yet. We also change in another way – and that is spiritually. Our spiritual growth is something that can be a private matter between ourselves and whatever we place our spiritual attention upon. It can also be a public affair – it can connect groups, build communities, create soul families and blend like-minded people together.

The thing with growth and change is that we have to symbiotically face an element of letting something go and leaving the 'old' behind. A simple analogy that I like to use is that when you get changed in the morning, you usually remove your nightwear first. The nightclothes are discarded and you choose a fresh set of clothes to start the day in. When we go through changes, at any level, we are automatically stepping into something new, and walking away from something old. When we go through changes that are much more significant and major, we have to let go of things that are equally significant and major, and as each change increases in its significance, the loss we face is also greatened. This movement and progression through life is natural, but brings with it a process that we may not necessarily be aware of or indeed ready to face.

Every change, loss or ending has a period of adjustment attached to it. This adjustment on lots of occasions is autonomous, where we rebalance and resettle into the 'new' with no problems and no drama. However, sometimes the adjustment is so great that if we are not aware of the need to acknowledge it, we become confused at our 'reaction'.

An example that comes to mind as I write this is very poignant to me. I used to be in a long-distance relationship. My partner used to live in London, over a hundred miles away from me in the Cotswolds, and due to circumstances, we were only able to see each other every couple of weeks. Even though this does not sound like a big deal, it really seemed to be a huge deal in *my* head. For three years, every other weekend we would spend a couple of lovely days together, and then have to say goodbye again. For a few days after this I felt very desperate and illogical feelings started to kick in, and I was unable to understand what was going on. It was only through writing this chapter that I realised each time he got back on the train after the weekend, and as I waved him off, it felt like I was saying goodbye again to something that I loved, and even though there was no death involved, my irrational mind linked these two concepts of saying goodbye and death together, and this triggered the emotional grieving process every time.

To add insult to injury, I realised a long time later that what I was feeling was also my own grief at leaving my hometown – London. I was born and brought up in London, and my roots were very much in West London, where I was raised and lived until I very suddenly decided to relocate with my ex-husband to the Cotswolds. This was (in theory) a lovely place to live and a great place to bring up our boys, who were just about to start full-time school. So, on paper, this move was idyllic and we were envied by many of my family and friends stuck behind in the 'rat race'.

However, I was a city girl with very bad hay fever, who disliked animals and had absolutely no inclination to start riding horses or going for long rural walks in the countryside; and was not happy about the shops shutting at 5pm every day. It was suddenly not such a great move, once reality hit home.

What had happened to my 24-hour fast-paced media lifestyle? Everything had changed so quickly. I felt cut off from my identity and my world. I felt like a fish out of water and this 'grief' manifested itself when my partner went back to the London that I had left and actually loved. Part of me wished I were going back there too – to the world I knew so well. I desperately wanted to be part of that 'rat race' again – it was what I knew. I wanted to get on a commuter-packed Tube train again, just to remember what it felt like to be a human sardine. I know it sounds ludicrous, but it was what I held as familiar, the only connection I had to my mum and dad, and to being their baby. But I had to move on: I had to stop being a child, and very quickly transition into being a parent. This was one of the hardest changes of my life. This was called growing up.

Once I realised that with all my 'goodbyes' every time he boarded that train I was grieving, it started to make sense to me, and I saw it for what it was. This didn't make it better; it just helped me to understand that I wasn't slowly going insane: I was just learning to accept the sudden changes in my life and move into acceptance. I had to look for all the good things about slowing my pace down. Maybe if you are reading this as a rural person born and bred, you are thinking I am mad to crave city life, but this had been my world for 35 years: London was where my root system had been established and cultivated. So of course adapting to the complete opposite would take time and start with grief, 'letting go', a movement into the new; slowly, but steadily, with ease and grace. It was not easy, but it was doable once I could see and identify with it.

7

SAYING GOODBYE TO MY FATHER

I was 24 years old when I had my first direct experience of death-related grief as I lost my father and wise mentor to leukaemia.

In his prime, he was an exotically youthful, beautifully charming automobile engineer, an avid reader and writer, a sportsman, a lover of arts and culture and a dynamic traveller. He soaked up his new continental and European experiences like a sponge broadening his Calcutta-born horizons. His travels took him West from India, to West Germany and eventually brought him to settle in West London, where he romantically met my young, shy mother at a bus stop in Hounslow East. I was his only little girl, and the apple of his very strikingly stunning green eyes. He protected me, advised me, counselled me, cajoled me and was living his life vicariously through me.

He had his first major myocardial arrest, commonly known as a heart attack, when I was only three years old. This shocking event immediately put him out of action as an engineer and he was under medical orders to change his lifestyle drastically. He had to leave the job he loved, modify his eating habits, stop smoking instantly and start regular exercise. However, these efficient action steps, very sadly, did not prevent the further attacks from happening. Unbelievably, he had another one every few years until he reached a record number of eleven by the time he died.

As a child, I became accustomed to the frequent blue-light trips in the night-time ambulance to Accident and Emergency, my dad strapped into a rapidly moving hospital on wheels that raced through the streets, in between the humming machine that records the heartbeat and the oxygen cylinder, watching each line on the monitor oscillate and hoping and praying that it would 'just keep moving'. Observing the rise and fall of his delicate chest, and willing him to keep that breath flowing. I eventually became desensitised, and stopped reacting nervously to the blue flashing lights that signalled danger and emergency. The urgent, blaring sirens became a familiar sound that was in its own strange way rather comforting. I calmly witnessed the resuscitation pads make an appearance many times and learnt that a short sharp shock can bring life back from death. So, there it was: shock is a good thing, it saves lives. I was not a professional therapist then, however, I was just a child – a child who learnt very quickly to adapt to the environment she was subjected to.

I got used to my clever and hugely resourceful dad getting 'better' from every one of these horrific episodes and just bouncing back, coming home and resuming where he left off; the notion of death just kept getting further and further away. My dad was obviously completely resilient. He was a tough cookie and therefore absolutely immortal!

My belief in immortality was something that was actually shredded in front of me years later, into strips of harsh truths and bitter reality. One day, something started to eat away at his life, like a hungry caterpillar. The cancer in his blood crept in and circulated around his constant hurting heart. Watching him deteriorate and decline mentally and physically was so painful, and left me speechless. Where had the resilience gone? Why was this happening? The emotions that arose at every moment were better off suppressed, as they did not seem to be assisting me in my daily life. I had to be efficient, practical and sensible. I had to 'keep calm and carry on'. Every day had its routine.

At that time, I was working at the BBC in West London, which luckily was around the corner from the cancer hospital Dad was in. So, every lunchtime, I would make sure I was at his bedside to sit for 30 minutes and eat my lunch while checking in on his status. As my mum didn't drive, and lived over 10 miles away, every evening, after work, I would pick her up, and bring her back to sit with dad so we would all be there, together.

My dad sacrificed so much for me. I was his only daughter, and although he never said it out loud, his eyes glistened with pride when he looked at me. He was always there for me through everything, he never let me down; he was my 'well wisher'. I needed to be there for him through this time, where he was slipping into his own world of pain, confusion and silence.

I have always been a naturally chatty person, so when I announced at work one day that I was going to be doing a 'sponsored silence' for one day to raise money for the ward that my father was in, you can imagine the delight and extreme generosity of all of my colleagues! The sponsored silence raised just under two thousand pounds, which was an amazing achievement.

Once I had collected all the money, I decided to approach my bank and ask for a giant presentation cheque made out to the ward that my dad was in. They obliged, and I picked up the giant dummy cheque to present to the hospital that evening.

It was also that very evening, just after I had presented the cheque to the ward that my dad chose as his moment to leave us. It was the nursing handover time so there was a hive of activity around the ward. My dad was in a separate room, so we could shut the door to the buzz of the ward and that was nice. I had butterflies in the pit of my stomach, as if I could sense his energy departing. My dad's brother and sister-in-law had arrived and we had gathered inside the room in silence, almost as if all of us felt the same nervous feeling. It was quite unusual to have all of us there, together in that way. Part of me wished I had him all to myself, but the other part was so relieved to be surrounded by the family that meant so much to him. My mum and the rest of the family were at the foot of his bed talking in hushed tones as I positioned myself next to my dad and leaned my head in next to his so I could whisper a feeble private goodbye. His eyes fluttered open with a flicker of momentary recognition and then he exhaled sharply. I felt his last breath, warm on my cheek, and that was it, he was gone. It was 9pm on the 9th of September. This was the last 999 call I had to make for him.

This was my first up close and personal experience with death and I was totally unprepared for the billowing gust of grief that suddenly knocked me sideways. My dad's departure punctured my life. He was my skeletal system and his disappearance left me limp, lifeless and floppy like a rag doll. I had no idea how to manage this loss, and it came as a complete surprise to me how much of a crutch he was in my life – although while he was alive, I would never have admitted this! Without my father, I felt hollow, lost and alone.

The best thing I could set about doing was to build a new structure for my life in the only way I knew how. I had been taught that my career, my family life, my home and my relationship were solid systems that could be relied upon, so I continued to root myself into these apparently secure aspects of my life. During this time, I also became a mother of two beautiful boys. This certainly distracted me for quite some time, so I put my grief in a box and buried it away in a safe place, and then forgot it was there.

The grief was a dormant explosion of anxiety waiting to happen - It was a potential rocket in my system that only needed a slight change to set it off. It was like living on top of a silent time bomb, not able to hear the ticking. This shook my world, like an earthquake that scores very highly on the Richter scale. In contrast, I also experienced how grief can sneak in to the system and later on I understood for myself how it can very slowly leak out – leaving me feeling flat, depressed.

8

SAYING GOODBYE TO MYSELF

DIPTI TAIT

'There's no greater power than the power of goodbye.' These are the lyrics from the Madonna song playing on the radio to me as I write this chapter. She's right. Goodbyes are final, they are endings, and all endings need some sort of acknowledging. This acknowledgement is grief, and grief is powerful.

It's been seventeen years since my wonderful father passed away and four years since losing my loving mother, both to cancer. Two weeks after my mother passed away, as I was immersed in my grief, my dearest grandmother followed her only daughter, was also carried away by old age.

A few months later, a much-loved teaching assistant at my children's school passed away after a weary battle with cancer, and then shortly after, my children's class teacher, who was a creative inspiration to everyone she met, shockingly died of a sudden heart attack. She had no previous history or illness and seemed bright, active, fit and healthy. Recently, a teenage girl who we knew also passed away in the middle of the night from a sudden asthma attack.

Just over three years ago we sadly lost another very close member of our family, very prematurely to bone cancer after a long-drawn-out and very brave fight, and then two years ago, we received the unbelievable news that an uncle had been terminally diagnosed with many forms of cancer. He only had a few weeks left; he sadly and most shockingly died soon after. My ex father-in-law was also in the last stages of his life as he slipped away from us just after that; another victim of cancer. Since then, a few friends of the family have passed away, and more recently, my auntie did not survive a routine operation, and was taken from this world just as her beautiful granddaughter was born into the world.

It seems to be a one-in, one-out system. But why does it feel so unfair and tragic if it is simply a numbers game? It's almost too much to bear. How can we trust life at all if we are surrounded by so much death? I ask this question quite a lot, and the answer is never an obvious or loud one. It's a very subtle, tiny voice that whispers back to me in Yoda-like fashion, 'Trust, you must.' So, this is what I hang on to. Some may call this faith, some may call it hope, and others will call it stupidity or naivety. These are labels, and all I know is that as soon as I surrender to the feeling of trust and relax into it, I feel better. Acceptance, I have decided, is much nicer than despair.

It's not just the death of people in my life that has contributed to my recent sense of loss and despair, but within all of this, my marriage of almost 15 years broke down, which led me to move out of my family home and give up my family unit. While writing this book, I have also gone through a divorce, and so endings and loss seem to be rather active in my life right now.

These major endings are also attachments to security. The life that I had invested my time, energy and love into building, had all just fallen away from underneath me. I was now on my own, an orphan. No longer a daughter, a wife or part of a family unit. But I am still a mother. This crucial label of 'mother' has kept me going. I am taking responsibility for picking myself up, climbing out of the dark well of despair and moving into the light.

I go to sleep some nights in floods of tears. The last thing I shout out into the empty still darkness is 'Who am I?'

All these harsh endings and all this loss have shaken me, like a massive earthquake. The overwhelming grief has almost engulfed me in a rush of raw emotions. It's overwhelming, it's shockingly scary, it's lonely, it's sad. I am angry, guilty, in denial. These intense feelings are the recognised stages of grief, and I know that I must surf the waves of grief, or else I will drown in the sea of pity. I am a survivor. I will not drown.

This is the time for me to heal, to mend, to find the resources necessary for my own earth to be rebuilt and re-established. This is why through this adversity, loneliness, darkness and isolation, I can seek solace in the only thing that cannot leave me, cannot die on me and will always be with me.

This is *myself.*

This is my own inner spirit, who has been quietly and patiently waiting to be my only companion on my journey ahead.

The journey is an inner one, a deep exploration into my own soul. Who am I? Or rather who am I not? Where can I find this inner happiness, peace, bliss, joy and love that we are told resides within us all? This is my own personal journey into myself. It's a hero's journey, and it starts with the intention.

I am ready to face this journey now and take this challenge of a lifetime. 'Feel the fear and do it anyway' is a popular spiritual teaching that pops into my head as I write this. I am definitely feeling the fear, and I am finding my feet on terrain that is unpredictable, uncertain, uncharted. It feels like I am learning to balance on a wobbly jelly. This is a journey into no-man's (or woman's) land. Nobody has ever walked this path before. This is my path to walk, and mine alone. I cannot bring a friend (or phone a friend), a guide or a helper. I have to simply trust that all I need will be provided for, as and when I need it.

It feels like one of those computer games, where you go on a mission to accomplish a task, and you are tested, challenged, dissuaded, misinformed, misguided, thrown, banished. All you have in order to complete your mission are the tools that randomly pop up for you to use and you need to be ultra aware, with heightened sensitivity at all times. It's a dangerous place, but if you have your wits about you and your senses sharpened, you will defeat and conquer, push through the pain, get through the darkness, and accomplish the task. The only difference is, there is no pause button, no reset, no cheats. This is the game of life, and it's one battle that you have to fight all on your own.

All sacred texts, spiritual teachings and wise gurus and sages tell us that the answers and solutions are contained within, so, I am now on my mission and inner journey to find them.

I feel like Dorothy in *The Wizard of Oz*, following a yellow brick road, only my road isn't a solid surface, it's definitely not yellow, and I don't have a cute dog running along beside me. And I most certainly don't have any ruby slippers on. All I have is my faith, my trust, my intention, my willingness, my calling to leap or tentatively step into the unknown. Apparently, I am told that even though I cannot bring a friend with me to hold my hand and support me, if I take the first tentative step off the solid, physical surface into the dark void, there will actually be a guide waiting, an angel, a well-wisher; a spiritual satnav, if you like. This is a comforting thought, and comforting thoughts are the ones I must reach for. Grief is a lonely, isolating place – it's cold and dark and scary. So, when there is some comfort offered, we must open our arms and reach out to this offering and grab on to it as hard as we can. This is the way out, the incremental steps towards the hope that we can move into the phase of healing and acceptance.

I realise it is not just myself who faces all this loss, and in turn feel so desperately alone and isolated. It is a universal pattern that repeats in its natural cycle day in, day out. Just as people enter into our world, people also exit. It's like when we are born; we have an invisible best-before date imprinted on our bodies. We all have a shelf life, and when it's up, it's up. The cycle of seed, growth, maturity, reproduction, death is a pattern that repeats all around us, in human, animal and plant life, in the natural world and in our seasons. So, if it is so normal and natural, why is the 'death' part so difficult to accept? Why is death such a challenge in our Western world to come to terms with? We do not seem to be adequately equipped emotionally or mentally to cope or deal with this thing we label as grief.

9

THE AFTER
SHOCK

Even if you have been forewarned about the diagnosis of your loved one for several years, or your loved one leaves this planet in a sudden and unexpected way, the loss will still bring about a feeling of shock and/or denial. Denial or disbelief is also part of the shock process.

Neurologically, shock is a default setting that our brains go into to put us into a robotic mode. Our brain has to have a natural 'shock absorber' to prevent us from over reacting in a highly charged emotional way. When we are over emotional, we cannot get things organised or achieved, due to the high drama of how we are feeling. Shock is simply a protective state that allows us to disconnect from our emotions and deal with traumas, changes and death in a pragmatic, practical and organised fashion.

This is why, for example, we may be able to go through the memorial service and funeral and register the death and sort out the paperwork and bureaucracy in such a methodically organised manner. We can also find ourselves delivering a word-perfect eulogy with a feeling of detachment and calm clarity.

This state can also feel like we are sleepwalking through a dream. We are disconnected from our emotions to such an extent that we even question our unemotional state, and are confused as to how we can be coping so well, and we may wonder what is 'wrong' with us? Well, actually, nothing is wrong. In fact this is perfectly normal and to be expected. It's a stage we can in fact capitalise on. While we are so detached from the drama of the experiences we have had, we can use the presence of mind that this brings in a useful way and get as many things organised and sorted as we can. This sense of keeping active and busy will give us some purpose for a while, and this sense of purpose is again useful for releasing positive hormones such as dopamine and serotonin into the brain, and can be the catalyst we need to lift us through.

It is interesting that many of us, when we are in shock, display the coping mechanisms of somebody who has not been affected by the incident, and our brains and bodies almost mimic 'normalcy'. This period is usually short lived and wears off when the reality of the situation kicks in, and we are slowly faced with life from a different point of view.

Shock can mimic a feeling of apathy; it creates an illusionary distance from our every day reality. It can be useful for smoothing over the sharp edge of pain.

Once the shock subsides, it can feel as if you have been standing outside in the freezing cold, where everything in your system goes numb. Once we move into a warmer place, we can thaw out and the feeling returns back into our outer extremities, and our inner hearts. We begin to feel again, and this incremental awareness of our feelings brings with it a realisation that we are moving into another stage within the grieving process.

10

GUILT IS THE BAD COP

Guilt is like an invisible plague. It almost hits you out of nowhere. When it does surface for me, it feels like I have two personalities that take the stage, the dominant one being the one that lists all the things I didn't do, I didn't say; the things I did do, and did say. Its objective is not a neutral one: it almost has an agenda – an agenda to bring you down. It's like the bad cop who kicks you when you are down and keeps you from raising your face to the sun and seeing the glimmers of hope. We can get lost and twisted in the grip of this all-encompassing feeling. To me it feels like a like a vice squashing my spirit.

But then, somehow, for some reason or another, I am able to briefly look up, and notice a chink of light – of hope – of reason. I notice that there is a doorway out of this living hell. So, I am able to make a dash for it and escape the torture of allowing myself to be dragged down by the negativity, and then thankfully my non-dominant 'good cop' starts to take control.

This is the sensible, intellectual part of us that is able to make a positive and proper assessment of the situation. This part of our brain helps us understand that we are, and have only been doing, the best we can, and we 'know' that what we have been able to do was at the time 'good enough'.

From this part of our awareness, we are able to forgive ourselves; we begin to give ourselves a break and we feel relinquished of this harmful energy. The dawn begins to break, and the day starts afresh. Once we can see how the stages of grief are like passing states, almost like clouds that appear in our lives and then disappear, we begin to understand that we are always in control – even though we rarely feel like it.

The phrase 'this too shall pass' is very useful to repeat to yourself until you recognise the similar transitions for yourself.

The reason I chose the image of the sun and cloud on the cover of this book, is that the weather (especially the notoriously changeable British weather) is an excellent metaphor for the transitional qualities of our emotional mind. Emotional states drift in and out of our awareness, like clouds masking the sunshine. The air pressure increases and squeezes water droplets out of the clouds and we then have rain. The rain releases the air pressure, and then the sun dries up the clouds and we return to blue sky and sunshine. Sometimes there are no clouds to be seen, when other times there is no blue sky to be seen. But, the weather is changeable, and so are our emotions. One of my quotes from my grief diary is:

> Emotions are like clouds in my mind, I have
> to squeeze them out and allow the teardrops to
> rain, soon the storm will pass, clear my mind
> and I'll bask in the sunshine again.

A really good question to ask when the guilty thoughts sneak in is 'Are these thoughts true?' Guilt does not usually offer useful facts as evidence; it replays a negative version of events. It's important to remember that behind every bad cop, there is a good one.

11

SADNESS IS LIKE A SICKNESS

Sadness can be an overwhelming feeling that usually goes hand in hand with guilt. They are suitable bedfellows. Sadness can creep up slowly, almost like a sickness or infection that has invaded your entire being. It feels like there isn't a definite location of its origin or existence, it's just like a cloud that hangs over us, or a toxic tonic that has been poured into us that seems to pollute our thinking, feelings and experiences.

It is interesting to note that sadness is a state that one feels when we have a low level of a chemical neurotransmitter in our brain called serotonin. You have probably heard this chemical referred to as the 'happy hormone', and this is why.

When we produce a constant flow of serotonin, we are generally nice, happy, coping, brave little souls. One of the things that stop the flow of serotonin is depression. When we are feeling low, down, sad and miserable, the brain does not produce any chemicals at all. This is why it is important for us to be aware of what sadness, guilt, loneliness and depression can do to us. They can reinforce the grip of this vicious circle, and we can then find ourselves caught in its trap, with no obvious way out.

But there is a way out. This is simply by interacting. Interacting with the world, a friend, a therapist, a healer, a doctor, even this book. Once we force ourselves to make a connection with a source who can listen, be supportive, offer kindness or just a friendly gesture, this gives us a sense of hope that we are not alone, that we are cared for and that we are loved and cherished.

Our grieving mind needs support. This form of support is individual, depending on your personality. If you are a private person, then a resource like this book is an excellent support system, as it will be helping you make connections into healing and acceptance while you read it: you can heal in your own way and keep your grieving private.

However, if you happen to have a more vocal personality, you may have to talk things through and reach out more to others who may be feeling the same way. It can be a source of comfort to be part of a network that understands. However, there is a danger that we can make the mistake of 'over talking' about the grief. There comes a point where talking too much can also keep us stuck.

So, for you, you will need to ask yourself the very important question of 'Do I want to be where I am right now?' If the answer is yes, then that is fine. If the answer is no, then the **No/Yes Principle**, which I will explain in chapter 18, will help to explain how you can begin moving forward.

12

DENIAL AND ACCEPTANCE

The long and short of it is, that the opposite of denial *is* acceptance. Denial is a really interesting phase, as it can often begin a long time before any actual death has occurred. With the example of both my parents, even though we were given a diagnosis of terminal cancer, I still did not actually believe the hospital and/or doctors were right. I refused to accept that this was an accurate assessment of the condition, and really did think that they would both get better, snap out of it and bounce back to normal. However, there comes a point where the denial subsides and reality smacks you around the face and after the initial shock, eventually acceptance begins to take its place.

Looking back, I had a sudden realisation of both my parents' individual situations, which almost made me snap out of the denial stage and truly begin to accept what was happening. Once this feeling of acceptance had arrived, I felt a sense of empowerment as if I managed to take a few steps forward and recognised my own control over decision-making. I also really felt like I understood the needs of my parents, and was able to facilitate those needs in a consistent and measured way. I used the model that I will be describing in chapter 18, called the **No/Yes Principle**. I hope that this model can also help you move into your own version of acceptance and peace.

13

ANGER INCREASES OUR STRENGTH

Anger is an interesting emotion. I have found that because I am normally not an angry person, when feelings of anger come up, it's almost a surprise, and then I recognise the feeling as a foreign one. This momentary recognition eventually enables me to remember that this is not really 'me'; it's simply the grief consuming me in another one of its clever disguises. Anger is simply a primitive response for us to increase our strength. For example, the things that make us angry ignite our passion. If we were disinterested, we wouldn't care. We show anger because we care, because our values have been shaken, or our belief system has been rocked. Sometimes, when things change, this can provoke an angry feeling because we feel out of our depth, or we have stepped out of our zone of comfort, and the feelings of discomfort can make us feel under some sort of threat. Anger is therefore a useful tool to help us be sure we are heard or honoured or acknowledged. The opposite of anger is calm, and like a tantrum-fuelled toddler, when they get what they want, the anger instantly disappears. So, grief displaying as an angry reaction can perhaps be a cry for help, and when the help appears, we feel better.

When I was in training to be a clinical solution-focused hypnotherapist, the course was very intensive, but fascinating. It taught me a lot about how the brain works and this really helped me a lot. Educating myself around the workings and processing of the brain enabled me to detach from my own emotional mind and observe it from a higher place of intellect and distance. This gave me moments of clarity and wisdom that I will be sharing in the final chapter of this book. It helped me move towards knowing how I can get to the place of acceptance of death, loss and change. I learnt to reframe death, loss and change into a positive, which helped me look for the growth and the learning that were being offered. Death has certainly taught me how valuable and precious life is. I realised that I have a choice to carry on living, as I am lucky enough to still have a life to live. The journey through life is a bumpy one, but with good suspension and a secure seatbelt in place, the bumps are less obvious!

There are many references within this book to the brain and the workings of it, as I really do feel that neurologically we can start to associate feelings with behaviours. We can begin to understand ourselves and the way we create our own neural pathways and connections inside our own brains, which influence how we think and feel, and thus, what we say and ultimately how we behave.

A few months into my hypnotherapy training, the senior lecturer mentioned death and the grieving process, and of course my ears pricked up, as I was very interested to hear his professional perspective on it, especially from a neuro-scientific understanding. He gave us what I thought (at the time) to be a very strange, explanation about how the intellectual part of our brain processes an emotional event like death. At the time of hearing this explanation, my state of mind was delicate and my grief felt raw, so my initial reaction was a wave of anger, but then, as I sat with this feeling and allowed it to subside, I was able to digest his theory. I came to an understanding that he may have had a well-executed point, and which I will go on to make in the next chapter for your information. It sometimes helps to see things from another perspective, and as we know, seeing things from a different viewpoint is very useful if we are to learn to detach from the drama of the situations we face and be able to move into the solution-focused place that is conducive to our healing.

When I experience any type of anger, I see the value of sitting with the experience and allowing it to surface in a controlled way. The analogy of a pressure cooker is very helpful here.

When something is bubbling away under pressure, it has got the potential to explode if the heat is turned up slightly more than normal. However, if we did not realise the pressure was building up and just let it build, we know that over time, this would be an explosion in waiting. The key to this pressure and this feeling of a slow build-up can be detected in this very useful emotion that we have labelled as 'anger'.

Anger and feelings of anxiety can be used as a very successful yardstick to measure the amount of pressure that has built up in the metaphorical pressure cooker that is your mind and body. When we notice the anger rising, we are able to make a choice as to how we release this pressure, so as not to cause an explosion. We are able to make an informed choice to release the valve in whatever way is best for us – this release has huge physiological benefits. We know that anger is a primitive response in the brain that reacts to a situation to increase our strength.

The important thing to remember here is that our modern day brain has two components: an emotional 'primitive' mind, and a much more evolved rational and 'intellectual' mind. So, if you think about it, even nowadays, when we have an overload of powerful emotions – like grief – it's not surprising that our thinking, perception and behaviour can switch into 'caveman/ woman' mentality.

When cavemen and women were alive, they were dealing with situations and issues that were actually life or death and they often experienced crisis or life-threatening conditions. This meant that they were probably very 'emotion' driven, rather than 'intellectually' driven.

The emotion of anger releases another chemical response in our brains that triggers the stress neurotransmitter noradrenaline, making us react quickly, sharply and with determination and a sense of boldness. That chemical is adrenaline.

The caveman/woman's world was an adrenaline-fuelled existence. They had to be constantly vigilant to ensure that they kept out of danger. Therefore, it is fair to assume that anger, fear or anxiety actually kept them safe and enabled them to remain in a constant state of 'fight, flight or freeze'. This state is also known as a more common word – **stress**. Stress for the cave dweller was very useful, as it induced a heightened awareness that prevented them from falling asleep and out of the tree into the middle of a pride of lions!

The difference between life as we know it today compared to the cave dweller's life, is that we have modern-day resources to keep us safe and protected, so we don't need this overwhelming emotional driver of stress to keep our senses switched to high alert. The thing to be aware of is that grief switches that high alert on for us, as our emotional mind is triggered; this is why we can sometimes feel as if we have lost our intellectual control.

It is interesting to note that fear, in just a small measure, releases the same amount of adrenaline into our system as anger. When we have a build-up of adrenaline in our delicately balanced system, we really need to release this to avoid repercussions to our physical and mental health. It's interesting to note that adrenaline is also released when we feel excitement or when we exercise. It can be utilised to keep us going or 'pumped up' to engage in the thrill, or to help us run away from danger. It's definitely a chemical that livens up our system and moves and shakes things up a bit. So we can use this chemical in a positive way, but if we allow it to sit idle and unused in the system, it turns into stress and then starts to spill out of the metaphorical 'stress bucket' in our brain and begins to pollute our body and our mind.

14

THE STRESS BUCKET

I mentioned that my lecturer said something strange about grief and at the time I perceived his comment to be rather controversial: 'Grief can be your best friend or your worst enemy'. In other words, we have a choice to either allow grief to grip on to us and pull us down or we learn to hold hands with it and use it as a support system.

However, now I have a much fuller and richer comprehension of how the brain works, as I continue to work with many clients in my busy hypnotherapy practice, I actually understand what he said, and because of this understanding, I also agree with it.

Grieving is actually a very stressful, overwhelming time, and includes all sorts of factors. Not only do we have to cope with our own emotional rollercoaster, but also, quite often there are other people whom we have to look after, manage, counsel and support – which adds to the stress. In some cases, there are no 'others', so the feeling of isolation and loneliness can also be a stressor.

There is a metaphorical part of our brain that we solution-focused hypnotherapists describe as the **'stress bucket'**. This is where our full range of mild to overly stressful events are stored and logged. This metaphorical bucket forms part of our primitive mind, which is the emotional mind.

Throughout our lives, as we go through our day, things can start piling into the bucket, especially when we feel a reaction like anxiety, fear or anger. These emotions are considered to be 'stressors'. As you can imagine, our buckets can get pretty full up if we are not careful and don't keep emptying it (pretty much like our household waste). When our buckets are full and spilling over, this has a pollutant effect on our mind and we can experience indicators such as feelings of depression, loss of intellectual control, catastrophic thinking, panic, phobia, a sense of being overwhelmed, paranoia and rage.

So, how do we empty the bucket? Luckily for us, our brain has a clever system in place. It's called REM sleep. When we go to sleep at night, we go through a stage called REM, which stands for Rapid Eye Movement. What we are doing in REM is very important and a key process to emptying our stress bucket. We are moving our emotional events, which are essentially 'emotional memories', from our primitive mind over to the intellectual part of our mind to be transformed into a narrative memory, a memory that is not linked to an emotional reaction.

For example, if you have a disagreement with somebody, and you are upset by it, you may think about it before you go off to sleep. When you fall asleep, in your REM sleep, you will re-run the event, either in clear pictures, where you may see, hear and feel the event playing through, or you may do it in metaphor, which is when you dream. What the brain is doing at this time is amazing and undeniably powerful! It is turning the event from an emotional event to a narrative event, so that when you wake up in the morning, you may just forget about it, or you will think about it and wonder why it affected you so much, as you suddenly feel better about it. This is why people say, 'Sleep on it', because sleeping on it empties the stress bucket!

Grief and the events surrounding it can also be contributing factors in this stress bucket inside our minds. So, in theory, if we know how to empty this bucket, this should help us move from overly emotional feelings towards an intellectual perception of the grief, therefore processing the grief appropriately.

My clients often understand this principle of the stress bucket, but the next question that usually follows is 'How do I empty my bucket?' This skill of **'how'** can be explained by remembering how the brain works.

So far, we understand that any outside factor that happens in our life is neutral until we become aware of it in our conscious mind. For example, when I was given the news that my father had leukaemia, and three months to live, I took the news incredibly well. This wasn't because I didn't care or that I am an overly rational person: it was because my brain went into a form of shock and/or denial, so that I could slowly absorb the words and reality of the information in a way that was not overwhelming for my system. Slowly, over the next few hours and days, this information began to sink in bit by bit. It felt as if it was bouncing in and out of my stress bucket. So, one day I felt broken into tiny little pieces, and then the next day I was able to get on with things as if everything was 'normal', and easily process the emotions that were appearing in my system without them creating a shutdown.

It was a confusing time as I ricocheted between being utterly devastated and upset, and hugely proactive and practical. This somehow enabled me to hold my life together and keep on top of things, to help my mother put plans into place and sort out my father's affairs with him before his decline, but then I would disappear and shut myself away and cry into the darkness and despair. It felt as if I had a split personality, but I now realise that it was my way of emptying the stress bucket, and finding my own sense of balance and neutrality. Even though I did not necessarily enjoy the feeling of grief, I allowed myself the permission to grieve and gave myself the 'choice' to resurface when I felt that I had 'emptied my bucket enough'.

Remember the stress bucket only has a small amount of memory capacity, and it fills up quickly with life events. So really, we as human custodians of our brain need to become aware of when the bucket needs to be emptied. This is what my hypnotherapy lecturer, describes as the brains ability to process emotional memories and convert them into narrative memories, because the narrative memory storage facility is more like the servers they have for Google!

Grief triggers the emotional memories, and then these emotional thoughts fill up our stress bucket. When our stress bucket is full, we have to be able to recognise this and take the necessary actions to prevent it from overflowing.

The example I give to my clients is that everyone has rubbish bins in their house. It is our duty to collect the rubbish weekly, and then put it out so that the refuse collectors can take it. If you forget to put your rubbish out one week, they will not be knocking on your door to ask for it. It is your responsibility to put your bins out!

In this case, when something huge has gone into your stress bucket, it is not advisable to ignore it and hope it goes away. It is really important that we take the action necessary to break it down, and we can only do this by recognising that our bucket has filled up.

The brain has its own natural ability to break down stress, as I explained, during REM sleep, but if we can understand that it is not only the events in our lives that can cause stress, but that our thoughts also play a huge part, then it's useful to question whether in some way we can help ourselves by learning to observe our own thoughts?

As I thought about it more and more, I realised that for me, the way I could help myself was not simply by trying to resist my stress, or to forget the experience or person I was grieving. It was more about how I learnt to turn the thought about the person and my experience into narrative, more positive memories: that made me feel good, rather than holding on to the negative emotions, which that made me feel bad. I realised, very dimly, that I had a choice to feel okay versus not okay. And in the times I did not feel okay, I moved into an acceptance of that feeling, and suddenly the not feeling okay became okay too!

The most liberating and useful thought I had was 'It is okay not to feel okay.'

This choice for being okay with not being okay may not be obvious, but I am suggesting that it's something you can look out for, because this leads to acceptance.

So, we must remember this simple skill. It may not be easy, but it is doable with the right training. Another useful quote to keep at the forefront of your mind: 'I always have a *choice* to reach for a better-feeling thought.'

There are some very basic practical ways to feel better. Remember I talked about stress causing a build-up of adrenaline into our system, which in turn fills up our stress bucket, causing the bucket to overflow? Well, the quickest way to release the adrenaline is to take a leaf out of Taylor Swift's offering and literally 'Shake it off'!

There have been many studies, and scientists all over the world have reported and demonstrated the hugely positive effects of exercise and physical activity on the neurochemistry of the brain. This doesn't mean that we should all sign up for gym membership: it can be any form of physical activity that simply helps to break the negative states that we can slip into, almost without noticing. Activities such as just popping out for a coffee to meet friends, or a little bit of window shopping, or a bike ride or a run round the park, even a short walk with a dog or a drive in the car, can help shift you into a positive frame of mind. There are three 'P's that keep us in balance, and when we attend to these three basic principles, we find ourselves maintaining a good headspace.

15

THE THREE PS

As this is a practical book, this is a good time for you to do a little bit of self- evaluation. Here is a practical task for you to complete. Write down on the following pages something small that you can do or think about that enables you to make sure all your '3 Ps' boxes are ticked.

The 3 Ps:

1. POSITIVE THOUGHT ..... ☑
2. POSITIVE ACTION .... ☑
3. POSITIVE ACTIVITY ...... ☑

I also want you to write down when you will aim to complete the task by. So, this starts to formulate into your personal action plan. This will help you find your own solutions for keeping you in a good frame of mind and moving you into a better headspace.

MY POSITIVE THOUGHT IS ..... ☐

MY POSITIVE ACTION IS ..... ☐

I will do this by ... _____

MY POSITIVE ACTIVITY IS ..... □

I will do this by ... _____

16

THE IMAGINED LEMON

The brain cannot tell the difference between imagination and reality. When we think about something, we have to imagine it; when we imagine something, we usually have to experience it through our feelings; and when we feel something, it becomes our reality, and then this reality confirms our initial thought and we believe it or reject it. This is what I describe as a thought-created belief loop. If you think about it, a belief is simply a thought that we think in a repetitive way. It's a thought that we keep thinking, and therefore because we keep thinking it, it becomes a 'fact' in our minds.

This is how it works. Here is a very quick exercise for you to try. Read the whole exercise through and then give it a go.

The Lemon Exercise

1) Close your eyes and imagine you have on a chopping board in front of you a big juicy Sicilian yellow lemon.
2) Imagine you are cutting this lemon in half and see the pips, the segments and the vibrant yellow of this lemon and start to notice the juice running out of it.
3) Then I'd like you to imagine that you are cutting the lemon into a quarter.
4) And now imagine as vividly as you can, that you are putting the quarter up to your lips and you can start to taste the sharp lemon juice inside your mouth activating your saliva glands.

What happened to you? Did your saliva glands activate? If they did, then this shows how our imagination can almost trick our senses into a response or a reaction to a *perceived* scenario rather than a *real* scenario.

This is why it is important for us to learn how to use the positive visualisation principles and tools to be able to activate our very powerful imagination centres in a beneficial way, to be able to move ourselves into a better-feeling space.

The first solution-focused question towards a better-feeling space is **'If I felt better right now, what would that feel like, and how would I know I'm feeling better?'**

17

MOVING INTO EMOTIONAL INTELLIGENCE

You now understand that we have two centres of thought: the 'emotional' mind and the 'intellectual' thinking mind. These two minds are certainly very different operating systems, but it is essential that they work together because they are not designed to operate in isolation.

In a very basic example, if we stopped using our emotional mind, then we would be displaying psychopathic or sociopathic tendencies. So, if we never got angry or upset, or fearful or even empathic about any situations or experiences, we could be viewed as robotically insensitive or an uncaring person, and this may cause conflict with the relationships we have.

However, if we only used our emotional centres, then we would be displaying tantrum-like behaviour and would over react to situations. Because emotional reactions are so dramatic, this would cloud any rational behaviour; this is when we may get into situations where we lose sensible control and regret our reactions.

To get the best balance, ideally we really need to be able to control and regulate ourselves to know how to get a harmonious equilibrium between the two centres and find our way into a space of emotional intelligence.

A space of emotional intelligence is where we are able to use our emotional indicators to allow us to know how to tailor the emotional reactive centre to get the rational, logical and reasoning mind on board to offer a response that would be considered 'measured' and 'reasonable'.

The emotional mind is designed to be reactive. This is because it has a simple function: to protect and preserve. Essentially it is our 'primitive mind' that is on the lookout for threat and danger so that we are alerted towards safety and security. It is a negative mind and will only give us the 'worst-case scenario'. The reason for this is simple. The function of the emotional mind is to keep us 'safe', but remember, it has no intellect, which means it cannot actually differentiate between a real threat and a perceived threat. So, this is why, when we are emotionally driven, *everything becomes a negative*.

Have you ever been in an argument with a person and you get over emotional, and suddenly you get this amazing negative checklist inside your mind that helps you list all the bad, annoying and irritating things that this person has ever done to you, and quite fantastically you are able to launch into a very personal attack that can sometimes appear like rapid gunfire?

This is the emotional mind working at its best. It has an impressive ability to fire bullets as a protective measure so 'you' remain unscathed. And, at the time, it seems as if these bullets are very important and it is necessary to fire them out in this uncontrolled way, and somehow once it starts, the trigger is pressed and you can't seem to stop until you run out of ammunition. The only problem is that when you regain rational control, you realise that you have shot down a situation or a person, and there usually are severe repercussions for that level of emotional outburst.

Luckily, as we have evolved as a species, we have grown an intellectual mind over the top of our limited primitive mind. We are able to show compassion, listen, understand, grow, learn, adapt and move towards change and innovation via the creative and expansive nature of the intellectual mind. This gives every human being the potential to help them move towards solutions, positivity and the possibility of a compelling future through hope.

The brain is designed to be able to change and adapt to the environment it is in, due to the neuro-plastic qualities within it. This essentially means that the brain is similar to 'Play Doh':

it can be moulded through our thinking, behaviour, beliefs, actions and experiences. Once we become aware of our brain's ability to adapt through experience, we are then in a powerful position to recognise that we can change our brain, simply by changing our experiences.

18

THE NO/YES PRINCIPLE

In this final section I will be giving you an insight into a model that I have developed called the **No/Yes Principle**.

This principle is a practical test to recognise initially that there is the desire to change and then work out the steps towards the change, using the emotional and intellectual minds, with awareness of the basic mechanics of the two systems. This principle will help you learn to observe the emotional signals of the brain in an intellectual way so that you are always in control of your mind and can be the driver of your own mental state.

Often, we cannot change our experiences, especially ones surrounding grief, loss or change, but what we can do is change our thought processes surrounding these experiences. Grief isn't something we can simply 'fix' with a tool or a principle, but it is certainly something we can learn to identify, be aware of and learn to manage. It is not about pushing it to one side, or ignoring it. It's about seeing it for what it is and acknowledging it, and then using the principle as a diagnostic indicator to observe it from the side-lines, if that's what you want.

The most important skill I teach my clients is 'thought management'. This helps them understand that they all have control over their thoughts, even if it doesn't feel like it. 'Thought management' is a skill for life that we can develop with strategies in place. My clients then discover for themselves their abilities to detach from their own thoughts enough to maintain the grip on intellectual thinking. It's about controlling your own mind, and knowing how to keep the control maintained.

Once we learn this 'thought management' skill, first with awareness, then with practice and repeated over time, we can move into noticing that we are the thinker, and therefore completely responsible for the thinking that we do. We then find that this has a positive knock-on effect on how we feel, which then influences our behaviour and ultimately the perception of our experiences. Sometimes, it can also happen the other way around, where a feeling will happen and then a thought will follow. It's debatable about what comes first – a thought or a feeling. Many argue that thought (conscious and subconscious) precedes feeling, but others argue that feelings create thought.

I have my own theory, and believe it can be both, depending on where we are 'hanging out' in our brain. When we are more intellectually driven, we are likely to be thinking first before feeling, but when we are more emotionally driven, we will be feeling before we think. Why does it matter to be able to identify this? It's a bit of a chicken and egg question, but I think that once we know which part of our mind is overactive, either emotionally or intellectually, we can use the thinking/feeling ratio as an indicator to move ourselves back into a state of balance and harmony quicker and with ease and grace.

We have an emotional scale that looks a bit like this:

Bored > Factual > Intellectual > Neutral < Rational < Passionate < Hysterical

There are some key questions that link to the **No/Yes Principle** that I ask myself in any given situation when I want to be able to quickly assess where I am on my personal emotional scale.

1) Is my current feeling useful?
2) Do I want to change how I am feeling?
3) What feeling do I want to move towards?
4) What small thing can I do to move towards the preferred feeling?
5) How will I know when I am there?

If I answer Question 1 with a **No**, followed by a **Yes** for Question 2, then I know I have got off the starting blocks for the No/Yes Principle to work.

The self-healing process always begins when a person can recognise that they want to change. It's not necessary to know what or how to change at that stage, it is just useful to know that something has to change. Once somebody has recognised this for him or herself, then this is the first entry point into the journey towards the solution.

In our hypnotherapy sessions, I ask my clients an interesting question called 'The Miracle Question'. This is a question that helps us identify what the goal is for the client. So, for example, if I asked you the first question followed by the second:

1) Is your current feeling useful?
2) Do you want to change how you are feeling?

And you answer no and then yes, I would then ask you to tell me what you want by asking you to imagine that a miracle happens, and you shut your eyes for a moment and a magic wand gets waved and then when you open your eyes again, you will be feeling exactly as you want to be feeling. How would you know? What will have changed? You will probably tell me that you are feeling better, and I will prompt you and ask you to describe the 'better feeling'. At this point you will be starting to answer Question 3.

3) What feeling do you want to move towards?

Once we have identified the feeling you wish to move towards from Question 3, we can then start to establish the small steps and action steps towards that feeling with Question 4. Because the solution-focused outcome is important to remember, we also check that this is at the forefront of the mind by asking Question 5.

4) What small thing can you do to move towards the preferred feeling?
5) How will you know when you are there?

Questions 3, 4 and 5 require a little more thought. Let me give you an example of how they are usually answered in the beginning, and how we move towards the solution or the preferred outcome.

When I have a new client in my hypnotherapy practice and I ask them how they *want* hypnotherapy to help them. They will usually answer in this sort of way: 'I *don't want* to feel the anxious feeling in my tummy when I wake up, I *don't want* to feel lonely or I *don't want* to be unhappy any more.' They may think that they have adequately answered the question, but actually they have told me what they *don't want*.

People, when unaware of the power of their thought 'requests', are used to telling themselves (and others around them) what they *don't want*. However, what I am trained to help them discover for themselves is how to move towards the solution, and invariably this is a scenario that they *do want*.

So, my question to you is: **What do you want?**

Usually, my client's answer will be along the lines of 'I want to feel "normal" or "happy" or "like the old me" again.' It's as if they know how to describe what they want from a familiar place of once having that feeling in the past, but the conflict arises from the fact that their life has changed, so they become removed from their past reality and they cannot perceive recreating what they once had. However, my job is to help my clients see that history is a great teacher: we can learn from the past, but it cannot always be recreated in the future. However, what we hope to be able to do is reconstruct another (more positive) version of it by starting with the simple-sounding question 'What do you want?'

It seems like a fairly innocuous question, but when most of my new clients are faced with it, it seems as if I have asked them to quote me convoluted passages from Shakespeare. They attempt an answer, but end up repeating what they don't want. I continue to ask them to tell me what *do* they want. They eventually get into it and then give me a proper answer, and this is the first step on their beautiful journey into their own compelling solution-based future.

So, Questions 3, 4 and 5 are the fundamental questions that kick-start healing and move you towards solutions. They serve to move you into helping you identify what you *do want*. What emotions *do* you *want* to be feeling? And, to check how you will know you are moving in the right direction is by noticing what changes you have actually made in *your actions* as you move towards your solution-focused outcome.

19

THE ONWARD JOURNEY

This book has been about my own emotional and intellectual journey into exploring the mechanics of grief, how the brain reacts to change and how best we can understand the journey. I have learnt for myself that there has to be a balance between allowing the grief a stage, and not perhaps giving it a microphone.

By sharing my journey and story with you, I hope that I have given you the opportunity to develop your own valuable insights, through reading this book, and that you can apply the skills and the awareness needed to get you through the tough times. Perhaps this book has been a trusted companion for you and you can continue to carry it around with you to dip in and out of if you need a boost or a top-up to provide you with a helpful answer wherever it flicks open for you.

It's my wish above all that you always know that you are not alone, and that this companion will guide you to feel better, or even if you don't feel better, feel content with how you feel and remember that our feelings are like clouds in the sky. They eventually pass over and there are breaks in the cloud where we get the glimpses of sunlight and remember that lovely feeling of warm sun on our faces as the tiny muscles in our faces begin to relax and soften. These are lovely moments of silence and stillness, where we do remember what peace feels like. We can start to hold on to these moments and learn to lean into them for support and nourishment. Our brain and our body develop a connection into this familiar positive space, as again, with practice and consistency, we begin building a new, self-correcting habit, almost like our very own root system whereby we learn how strong and resilient we are.

It is during those times when we feel low, that we gain in power. We can learn to use our inner power to root ourselves into empowerment. It's not easy, but it's doable. It takes time and commitment, and like any habit, the more you do it, the easier it becomes.

This delicate balance between tiptoeing out of the primitive mind and dancing into the intellectual mind is a skill that we have to learn and practise.

Recently, one of my clients told me that he had made some modifications to the 'dark cave inside his mind'. He has installed big bay windows into the cave wall, overlooking the bright and 'happy' beach that he used to go to as a child. He says that when he feels like the caveman mentality has taken over and he feels stuck inside his cave, he knows that it has a much better outlook and remembers that it's his choice to remain stuck in the dark, or to make the choice to step outside onto the bright, warming beach. Again, to reiterate, it's about discovering for yourself the choice you have to 'reach for a better-feeling thought'.

I would like to think that this book has helped you think about things in a different way, one that allows for feelings to surface and subside in an appropriate way for you, and that it has been a comfort to you to know that you are certainly not alone.

Once you know the skills, it isn't as simple as just applying them once and that's it. The brain and the mind are very organic structures that operate and change on a moment-by-moment basis, so this form of mind management takes knowledge, skill and practice. It is the practical application of the skills and knowledge in the form of discipline and commitment that keeps us buoyant and keeps us habitually surfing the waves of grief and understanding that sometimes a tidal wave will come out of nowhere, but the skill is to find the surfboard and climb back on, regain balance and composure and learn to enjoy the ride of your life. And, good grief, it's definitely an interesting journey.

The healing happening inside you may not be evident just yet, but a lot happens under the surface of our subconscious mind that we may be unaware of consciously ... Which reminds me of a little story that I would like to share with you.

It's a story about a little three-year-old boy named Jacob who came home from nursery one day with a small plastic cup filled with earth, with a label marked 'Look after me'. His mummy asked him what was in the pot. Jacob replied, 'It's my sunflower seed. I have to water it and look after it and it will grow even bigger than me.'

His elder brother Krishan was listening and incredulously asked how a tiny seed could grow bigger than his brother.

Jacob shrugged his shoulders and said he didn't know, but he knew he had to water it.

A few hours later, Jacob and Krishan's mummy found them both staring into the pot of earth on the windowsill and she asked them what they were doing. They replied in unison, 'Waiting for the sunflower to grow!' The mummy laughed and explained that the seed would take time to grow.

The following day, she found them both in the same place staring into the little pot, and again asked them what they were doing, and again, the same reply came back: 'Waiting for the sunflower to grow.' The mummy then explained that the seed was under the surface doing a very special and important job: it was busy making a root system. She explained that if the sunflower was going to grow bigger than them, then it had to have a way of supporting itself and making sure that it will not fall over and stay strong and tall.

She continued to tell them that all the work to build the root system was happening under the surface, and that when it was ready and it knew it had done enough root building, the little seedling would emerge. It would then grow really fast and really high. The boys then understood, and knew that they still had to keep watering and looking after the little seed, even if they couldn't see any evidence of it yet.

Thank you for joining me on my journey through grief. Like the sunflower, the idea of writing this book was a little thought 'seed' and my dedication and commitment to this topic has been a way of nourishing my own grief and helping it to grow and evolve into something that I can harmoniously live with. Like the ivy I described at the beginning of the book, it's a climbing plant that can easily take over if we are not aware of it, but it can also be beautifully trained and cultivated to grow in places that fill in the holes and gaps that grief can leave behind.

I feel like I have learnt enough and taught myself how to be the positive 'gardener' of my own grief and have accepted that I will not simply 'get over' grief, or simply ignore it and hope it goes away, but can now be in a good place in my mind to be able to invite it into my life. I also have learnt to remind myself of the liberating choice that I have to be able to transform it. I hope that my journey has helped you get enough 'evidence' you need to be able to transform your own grief into good grief.

NOTES TO SELF

NOTES TO SELF

NOTES TO SELF

NOTES TO SELF

NOTES TO SELF

NOTES TO SELF

NOTES TO SELF

Printed in the United States
By Bookmasters